The Ten G̲ ̲ ̲ ̲ ̲ ̲ ᴜᵢ ᴛʜᴇ Bible

By Benjamin L. Reynolds, M.Min

Discover other titles by this author at http://www.benjaminlreynolds.com
and discover other titles at http://amazon.com/author/benjaminreynolds

Other titles by Benjamin L. Reynolds

Seven Years until Eternity: The Rise of the Antichrist
Sons of God Daughters of Men
Ready for the Rapture
Living in the New Millennium and Beyond
40 Days of Faith
The Penny
The Ten Greatest Prayers of the Bible

Copyright © 2012 by Benjamin L. Reynolds

ISBN 10: 978-1478137719

ISBN 13: 1478137711

Table of Contents

Introduction

The Bible contains over one hundred and fourteen miracles in six categories, including the human body, nature, military intervention, food, animals, and finances. Sixty-two of these miracles involve the human body; twenty-nine involve nature and eleven describe the miraculous provision of food. The once incurable disease of leprosy was cured four times and paralysis seven times. Healings were performed on one person, several people at once(ten lepers in Luke 17:11-19) and an entire army. (the Syrian army in 2 Kings 6:8-20) Most people were healed while in contact with an anointed person of God, but a some were cured after touching inanimate objects. (2 Kings 20:1-11, Acts 19:12) In short, the Bible is full of many miracles occurring in many ways.

Miracles happen when we least expect them, but need them most. Merriam Webster's dictionary defines a miracle as "an extraordinary event manifesting divine intervention in human affairs and an extremely outstanding or unusual event, thing, or accomplishment." As we read about miracles in the

Bible, how many of us ask if these same miracles could take place today? If God is the same today, yesterday, and forever, (Hebrews 13:8) then why are we not seeing great miracles like the parting of the Red Sea or thousands fed with a few pieces of bread and fish? God has not lost the willingness to perform great miracles, but rather we have not presented him with the opportunity to manifest large scale, attention-grabbing miracles of faith.

Miracles should not be limited to people in the Bible who showed great faith. We should be able to feed thousands of people as Jesus did. We should be able to sway the hearts of unbelievers and pagans by manifesting the power of God in the sight of the nations as Elijah did. We need the courage to stand righteous in the midst of political persecution, intolerance, and manipulation like Daniel, Shadrach, Meshach, and Abednego so that God can prove himself through our resolute faith. In our modern era of science, medicine, and technology, WE NEED MIRACLES to do what arguments and debate cannot!

I wanted to achieve several things by writing this book. First, I wanted to show the importance of believing in miracles. As I have written in other books, I owe my life to the miracles God has performed in my body to heal and sustain me. I have also been privileged to have the Lord do miracles in and through me. I know firsthand that believing in and seeking after miracles invites the opportunity for divine intervention into our human affairs. Second, I want readers to understand that but we do not have to accept the status quo of the world around us. Through our faith in Jesus Christ, we have the ability to manifest supernatural miracles and change what many believe is unchangeable. All we have to do is understand what miracles are and how to manifest them. The people in the Bible who received miracles were not different from us. By exercising the key elements of faith, humility, obedience, and sacrifice, they were able to manifest the kinds of miracles that we dream of seeing today. We can achieve these same results by examining what certain people in the Bible did to see miracles and looking at the specific ways they exercised faith.

I began my study by examining every miracle in the Old and New Testaments. After doing so, something extraordinary stood out:

1. Most miracles in the Bible occurred when people had no other option but to trust in God. People will usually only turn to God for a solution after they have exhausted every available option

2. Virtually every person in the Bible who experienced a miraculous event exhibited four basic characteristics before receiving their miracle:

   a. Humility

   b. Obedience

   c. Sacrifice

   d. Determination

I did not write this book with the intention of trying to say that the miracles selected in this book were better or have more spiritual significance than those not selected. In making my selections, I choose miracles that I felt were simply more outstanding and influential at the time they occurred and as time has passed. I began my study by creating a list of every miracle in the Bible where someone believed in God to do something miraculous. I then narrowed the list down by looking at the overall results of each miracle. To me, the most important aspect of each miracle were the overall results. Great prayers can, and should be, judged by their results. Every miracle in the Bible is significant, but I believe that some miracles had a greater effect than others and wanted to understand why. I then created the following criteria list for what I believed were the twenty-five most outstanding miracles in the Bible.

1. **Impact:** This is a measure of how many lives affected by this miracle. More weight was given to miracles that affected more people.

2. **Repeatability:** A measure of how likely an ordinary person is to be able to repeat this miracle. Since the Bible tells us that every person is given a certain amount of faith, (Romans 12:3, Luke 17:5) repeatability indicates how much faith might be required to duplicate the same results. A low score on the repeatability scale is not to say that a person could not repeat this miracle, only that a great deal of faith would be required.

3. **Other available options:** A measure of whether or not the person or persons involved could have chosen another avenue and achieved similar results.

4. **Awe Factor:** Over the years, how many people reading about this miracle have been in aw of it.

I chose not to rank the miracles in a list from one to ten because I believe that doing so would devalue the significance of each. Every miracle selected was great in and showed unique insights into prayer, faith, the human character, and the character of God. I also would like to say that the person performing the greatest miracles would have to be Jesus Christ. Because of this, I chose miracles were someone other than Christ acted by faith to bring about the miracle in order to better illustrate how ordinary people can use practical methods to bring about miraculous results.

As we look at The Ten Greatest Miracles of the Bible, I hope that you will gain an appreciation for the power of miracles to change lives. I hope that you will understand there is no difference between us and the people who experienced these miracles. We have the same potential in faith, prayer, and can experience the same things people in the Bible did. In reading this book, you will gain insight into how you or someone close to you can experience the awe inspiring, wondrous power of God's miracles.

May God Bless you, and keep believing in miracles!

CHAPTER 1

Elijah Multiplies Oil and Meal for the Widow at Zarephath

The Miracle

"So he arose and went to Zarephath. And when he came to the gate of the city, behold, the widow woman was there gathering of sticks: and he called to her, and said, Fetch me, I pray thee, a little water in a vessel, that I may drink. And as she was going to fetch it, he called to her, and said, Bring me, I pray thee, a morsel of bread in thine hand. And she said, As the LORD thy God liveth, I have not a cake, but an handful of meal in a barrel, and a little oil in a cruse: and, behold, I am gathering two sticks, that I may go in and dress it for me and my son, that we may eat it, and die. And Elijah said unto her, Fear not; go and do as thou hast said: but make me thereof a little cake first, and bring it unto me, and after make for thee and for thy son. For thus saith the LORD God of Israel, The barrel of meal shall not waste, neither shall the cruse of oil fail, until the day that the LORD sendeth rain upon the earth. And she went and did according to the saying of Elijah: and she, and he, and her house, did eat many days. And the barrel of meal wasted not, neither did the cruse of oil fail, according

to the word of the LORD, which he spake by Elijah."
(1Kings 17:10-16)

Reason for Choosing this Miracle

While this miracle only affected a few people, it is extraordinary in the fact that God multiplied a one-day supply of oil and meal and caused it to last from one to three and a half years.

Background Information

God sent the prophet Elijah on a dangerous mission to deliver a message to Ahab, the king of Israel saying that there would be no rain until he decreed it. After delivering the message, God commanded Elijah to leave and hide by a brook at Cherith, where ravens would feed him miraculously. When the brook dried up due to no rainfall, God spoke to Elijah and told him to go to Zarephath, where a widow woman would take care of him.

Key Elements of This Miracle

1. *The woman exercised **HOS, (Humility, Obedience, Sacrifice)** three critical elements needed to receive a miracle.*

    a. *Humility* - The widow showed humility in two

ways. First, when Elijah showed up, he asked her to bring him some water. The woman must have thought, "Why can't he get his own water?" Rather than showing her displeasure, she kindly agreed. Second, Elijah asked her to bring him bread before feeding her and her son. Again, the man of God asks her for something she is in no way obligate to provide. Rather than getting puffed up or responding with sarcasm, the woman showed humility. How would you respond if someone asked you to take the last portion of food you have for you and your child and then feed him or her first? This woman's humility was remarkable in that the only denial she made was that she did not have any additional bread to offer the man of God.

b. *Obedience* -The woman showed obedience by doing exactly what Elijah asked. He was a stranger and she had no reason to trust him, but still followed his instructions. When asked to get water, she said yes. Elijah asked her for bread and she told him there was only enough

11

for her and her son. Elijah convinced the woman that by feeding him first, her and her son would be blessed with more. His request must have seemed ridiculous. She would have been well within her rights to deny him, but chose to believe and obey. When the man of God's directives seem absurd, we must have the spiritual foresight to see the spiritual benefit behind it if we are going to see a supernatural blessing.

c. *Sacrifice* – The woman sacrificed the small amount of meal and oil she had left to feed Elijah first and then her own family. Why anyone in his or her right mind would feed a stranger first, with no prospects for more food and only the promise that the food will not run out until it rains is beyond the grasp of most people. It was amazing that this Phoenician, non-Jewish woman believed that Elijah was a man of God whose prophetic words of blessing would come true if she took care of his needs first. By sacrificing a portion of her last meal, the woman revealed several important concepts:

i. Learn to be unselfish – As Paul once reminded, "I have shewed you all things, how that so labouring ye ought to support the weak, and to remember the words of the Lord Jesus, how he said, "It is more blessed to give than to receive."" (Act 20:35) God provides a special blessing for those who put others first and help the less fortunate.

ii. She knew there was a blessing in helping the man of God - In Genesis 12:3, God says that he will bless those that blessed Abraham, the man of God. Jesus explains the rewards of helping those who preach God's word in Matthew 10:41-42:

"He that receiveth a prophet in the name of a prophet shall receive a prophet's reward; and he that receiveth a righteous man in the name of a righteous man shall receive a righteous man's

reward. And whosoever shall give to drink unto one of these little ones a cup of cold water only in the name of a disciple, verily I say unto you, he shall in no wise lose his reward." (Matthew 10:41-42)

Anyone who gives assistance to the representatives of God will be rewarded according to their faith.

2. *Elijah, as a man of God, had to exercise* **HOS, (Humility, Obedience, Sacrifice)** *in order to produce the miracle.* This miracle is unique in that the person performing the miracle had to exercise the same traits as the person receiving the miracle. God positioned Elijah so that he would have the right attitude and be in the right place to meet the widow woman.

   a. *Humility* – Elijah, the mighty prophet who had recently gone before the king and prophesied it would not rain until he declared it, was reduced to begging a poor widow woman for bread and water. It must have been ironic and humbling that he had to endure the consequences of a drought he prophesied, but still he pressed forward without complaint.

b. *Obedience* – Elijah went to the city of
Zarephath, exactly as God told him. He was
not a disobedient prophet like Jonah or other
prophets. (Jonah 1:31, 1 Kings 13:1-26) By
obeying God's word, Elijah was in a position
to perform the miracle that sustained his
needs and the widow's for more than a year.
What a blessing when we obey God's word!

c. *Sacrifice* – By choosing to remain a prophet of
the Lord after he delivered his initial message
to King Ahab, Elijah was making a
tremendous sacrifice. He could have changed
his career, sold out his true calling, or did
something other that what God called him to
be. He chose to continue doing God's will.
This was not easy because King Ahab and
Queen Jezebel wanted to kill Elijah because
of his unpopular prophetic messages. (1
Kings 18:13, 19:1-2, 1 Kings 22:8,18) Why
would anyone want to be a prophet of the
Lord under those dire circumstances? Elijah
remained a prophet because he wanted to

serve God faithfully and return Israel to worshiping God in Spirit and truth. (1 Kings 19:14) What unselfish sacrifices the ministers of Lord make so people can receive God's blessings.

3. *God directed Elijah from one miracle to the next.* If someone is fortunate enough to experience one miracle in a lifetime, that is a great blessing. Elijah was blessed to experience one miracle after the next during his ministry. Before he met the widow woman at Zarephath, God miraculously fed him using ravens. After he performed the miracle of multiplying her meal and oil, he resurrected her son from the dead. After that, he miraculously called down fire from heaven, and so on until he had performed ten miracles. How was it that God used Elijah to perform so many miracles? It was because he lived a surrendered life. By exercising humility, obedience, and sacrifice, (HOS) Elijah was always in a position where God could work through him.

What can we learn from this miracle?

We can learn several things from this miraculous story:

1. Humility, obedience, and sacrifice (HOS) are key characteristics in receiving a miracle and allowing God to use you to perform one.

2. God does not require much to perform a miracle in our lives, multiply what we have, and supply our needs. This story tells us that even a poor person can seek God in prayer, ask what he can do to bless them with more, and then look at their lives to see what they can sacrifice. God multiplied the widow's one-day supply of oil and meal by a factor of hundreds. Not a bad return on her investment of faith!

CHAPTER 2

Elisha and the Shunammanite Widow's Unending Supply of Oil

———

"One of the wives of a disciple of the prophets called to Elisha, "Sir, my husband is dead! You know how he feared the LORD. Now a creditor has come to take my two children as slaves. " Elisha asked her, "What should I do for you? Tell me, what do you have in your house?" She answered, "I have nothing in the house except a jar of olive oil." Elisha said, "Borrow many empty containers from all your neighbors. Then close the door behind you and your children, and pour oil into all those containers. When one is full, set it aside." So she left him and closed the door behind her and her children. The children kept bringing containers to her, and she kept pouring. When the containers were full, she told her son, "Bring me another container." He told her, "There are no more containers." So the olive oil stopped flowing. She went and told the man of God. He said, "Sell the oil, and pay your debt. The rest is for you and your children."" (2 Kings 4:1-7) GWT

Reason for Choosing this Miracle

Although only a few people were affected by this miracle, there are several important reasons for choosing it:

1.   This miracle shows that God is concerned about our finances and can bless us so our obligations are met and we are financially self-sufficient.

2.   This miracle shows the principle of God requiring something from us, even if it is minuscule, to work a miracle in our lives.

3.   This miracle shows that the upper limits of what God can bless us with is only limited by what we can give him by faith.

Background Information

The prophet Elisha had recently succeeded his mentor Elijah as the lead prophet of a group of fifty men calling themselves the "Sons of the Prophets." (2 Kings 2:15) Elisha received a double portion of Elijah's spiritual anointing (2 Kings 2:9-10) and watched him taken to heaven by an angelic host. (2 Kings 2:11) When a woman whose husband was part of The Sons of the Prophets died, she came to Elisha seeking help. The widow came to Elisha because she was desperate to pay her creditors and avoid having her two sons taken into slavery as collateral. As the leader of the prophets, Elisha must have felt responsible to help this poor woman.

Key Elements of This Miracle

1. *God did not give the woman money, but blessed what she already had and could obtain by faith to provide the money to pay her obligation.* In 2 Kings 4:2, Elisha asked the widow, "What do you have in your house." He knew that the woman had probably already exhausted every financial option, so instead of looking for a financial solution, Elisha sought a spiritual one. He began by taking inventory of what was in her house to see what God would be able to use. Why did Elisha not pray for God to give her the money to pay her debts? The answer is simple. He understood that God does not give something for nothing. A recurring financial promise of prospering throughout the Bible teaches that for God to give you financial increase, you must first give him something of importance. **Sacrifice** is a crucial step in the

requirements of **HOS (Humility, Obedience, and Sacrifice)** Sacrifice is a necessary principle of tithing, offering, and miracles. What we give God does not always have to be an exchange of financial goods, but it should be something of importance to us. When Elisha discovered the widow had an empty pot of olive oil in her house, he decided that would be the starting point or her miracle.

2. *God took something finite and made it infinite.* We should never discount what we have to offer God because he can take our small sacrifice and multiply it into a lot. It does not matter what we have to offer God or how much we have when we offer something mixed with faith.

"For unto us was the gospel preached, as well as unto them: but the word preached did not profit them, not being <u>mixed with faith</u> in them that heard *it.*" Hebrews 4:2

Rich or poor, strong or weak, whether we have a lot or a little, God is looking to take what we bring him by faith and multiply it. Saying that we are poor or do not have enough is not an excuse! It takes faith to take what little we have and give it to God with no hope of return, but that is what faith really is!

"Now faith is the substance of things hoped for, the evidence of things not seen." Hebrews 11:1

If we exercise more faith and give God what we have available, then we will receive greater blessings.

A few years back, I visited a church and attended the prayer meeting before morning service. As I prayed, a man approached me and asked if I would take the money he had in his hand. Confused, I said no and walked away and continue praying. He returned a few minutes later and begged that I take the money he was offering. I grudgingly accepted only after he refused to take no for an answer. The man approached me again after the morning service, and asked if I would come with him to speak with his wife. I had no idea why this man kept bothering me, but agreed to go with him. When we arrived, the man thanked me for taking his money, then began crying. He said that he and his wife needed money to pay their electricity bill the next day or it would be shut off. During the Morning Prayer, God had instructed him to give me all his remaining money. He did so and by the time he returned to the pew his wife was sitting in, God had told someone to write her a check for the exact amount of their light bill, about five times what he had given me. I came to understand that day what God's principle of multiplication meant. If you do not have enough to meet an obligation, pray, and put all you have in his hands to see if the Almighty will multiply it.

The oil God miraculously provided to the widow did not run out until she and her sons ran out of pots to put it in. After they filled the last pot, the oil stopped. The scriptures make it clear that the maximum blessing God is able to provide is only limited by what we give him to work with by faith.

"Then touched he their eyes, saying,

According to your faith be it unto you." Matthew 9:29

"Having then gifts differing according to the grace that is given to us, whether prophecy, *let us prophesy* according to the proportion of faith;" Romans 12:6

If the widow could have brought fifty pots, then fifty pots would have been filled. The only limitation was what she was able to bring to God by faith. When we are in need of financial blessings, let us bring God as much as be can by faith as a down payment on what he will surely multiply and send back to us in return!

3. *The woman exercised* **HOS, (Humility, Obedience, Sacrifice)** *three critical elements needed to receive a miracle.* We discussed the widow's sacrifice of oil, but the *humility* and *obedience* she exercised were also critical to receiving a miracle. First, she had to humble herself and accept the instructions the man of God gave her by asking friends and neighbors for help. It must have been humiliating

24

to let friends and family know that her finances were in such disarray that her sons were about to be taken as slaves by the creditors! In addition, instead of giving her the needed money, Elijah told her that the solution to the problem would be in borrowing empty pots. At first thought, Elijah's instructions did not make sense. We have to understand that miracles do not have to make sense to us; they have to make sense to God. The widow received her blessing by exercising great humility and obedience as she faithfully followed Elijah's instructions.

CHAPTER 3

The Walls of Jericho

The Miracle

"Now Jericho was straitly shut up because of the children of Israel: none went out, and none came in. And the LORD said unto Joshua, See, I have given into thine hand Jericho, and the king thereof, *and* the mighty men of valour. And ye shall compass the city, all *ye* men of war, *and* go round about the city once. Thus shalt thou do six days. And seven priests shall bear before the ark seven trumpets of rams' horns: and the seventh day ye shall compass the city seven times, and the priests shall blow with the trumpets. And it shall come to pass, that when they make a long *blast* with the ram's horn, *and* when ye hear the sound of the trumpet, all the people shall shout with a great shout; and the wall of the city shall fall down flat, and the people shall ascend up every man straight before him." Joshua 6:1-5

Reason for Choosing this Miracle

This miracle was selected for several important reasons:

1. It shows what a group of believers can achieve if they combine their faith.
2. It shows the importance of patience while waiting on God for a miracle.

Background Information

The Israelites had spent more than forty years wandering throughout the Sinai desert after leaving Egypt as slaves. They were now ready to take the land of "milk and honey" promised to Moses and their ancestors. Standing in their way were the dreaded, fortified cities-states of Canaan, which their ancestors had doubted they could conquer. Joshua gave the Israelites a rousing speech after the death of Moses and miraculously crossed the Jordan River to fight against Jericho. Archeologist have discovered that the city's stone walls were fifteen-feet high, six-feet thick, and topped by another eighteen foot, freestanding mud brick wall. With virtually no military experience or siege equipment, Joshua and his army faced a daunting task.

Key Elements of This Miracle

1. *Joshua's army was augmented by God's spiritual army.* Joshua 5:13-15 says that Joshua had a supernatural visitor the

night before the siege of Jericho began.

"And it came to pass, when Joshua was by Jericho, that he lifted up his eyes and looked, and, behold, there stood a man over against him with his sword drawn in his hand: and Joshua went unto him, and said unto him, *Art* thou for us, or for our adversaries? And he said, Nay; but *as* captain of the host of the LORD am I now come. And Joshua fell on his face to the earth, and did worship, and said unto him, What saith my lord unto his servant? And the captain of the LORD'S host said unto Joshua, Loose thy shoe from off thy foot; for the place whereon thou standest *is* holy. And Joshua did so." Joshua 5:13-15

This "captain" of God's angelic army came to show Joshua that the Lord was on his side and that he would prevail. Many times we see an insurmountable task and doubt that God will give us success. We are unsure how to proceed because a great deal is at stake and failure may cause harm to us or someone else. What we need in those times is spiritual assurance from God. An angel, a word from God or the Holy Spirit can give us the necessary confidence to proceed. In Joshua's case, the angelic visitor confirmed that God was on his side. A deeper examination of the passage hints that the person who visited Joshua may have actually been God. Joshua 5:14 tells us that Joshua bowed to the ground and gave reverence. This act of reverence occurs in other places in the Bible:

> "And he said, Draw not nigh hither: <u>put off thy shoes from off thy feet, for the place whereon thou standest <i>is</i> holy ground. Moreover he said, I <i>am</i> the God of thy father, the God of Abraham, the God of Isaac, and the God of Jacob.</u> And Moses hid his face; for he was afraid to look upon God." Exodus 3:5-6

In Joshua 5:15, the visitor tells Joshua to take his sandals off because he was on holy ground. Moses was to remove his shoes when he first encountered the presence of God in the burning bush on Mount Horeb. Whenever someone in the Bible bowed to give reverence to an angel not representative of a true manifestation of God, the person was immediately told not to do so by the angel.

> "<u>And I fell at his feet to worship him. And he said unto me, See <i>thou do it</i> not</u>: I am thy fellowservant, and of thy brethren that have the testimony of Jesus:

worship God: for the testimony of Jesus is the spirit of prophecy." Revelation 19:10

We can therefore conclude that God visited Joshua the night before the siege of Jericho to assure him that his campaign would succeed and that the host of heaven were with him. This was not the only time that God let his servant know that they were backed by the armies of heaven. He did the same thing for Elijah when the king of Syria sent soldier to kill him:

> "And when the servant of the man of God was risen early, and gone forth, behold, an host compassed the city both with horses and chariots. And his servant said unto him, Alas, my master! how shall we do? And he answered, Fear not: for they that *be* with us *are* more than they that *be* with them. And Elisha prayed, and said, LORD, I pray thee, open his eyes, that he may see. And the LORD opened the eyes of the young man; and he saw: and, behold, the mountain *was* full of horses and chariots of fire round about Elisha." 2 Kings 6:15-17

Jesus boasted that a heavenly army was on standby to assist him:

"Then said Jesus unto him, Put up again thy sword into his place: for all they that take the sword shall perish with the sword. Thinkest thou that I cannot now pray to my Father, and he shall presently give me more than <u>twelve legions of angels?"</u> Matthew 26:52-53

God always has a spiritual army waiting to help his servants in the natural world.

2. *Joshua and the Israelites exercised* **HOS, (Humility, Obedience, Sacrifice)** *before receiving their miracle.*

    a. *Humility* - Before fighting, the Israelite soldiers were instructed to march around Jericho and wait on God. They willingly endured the frustrating and humiliating task of having the soldiers of Jericho look down from the walls and laugh as they marched silently around the city for seven days.

    b. *Obedience* -The Israelites had four distinct instructions given to them by Joshua:

        i.   March around the city once for six days then seven times on the seventh day.

    ii.   Maintain silence for six days then shout after circling the city the seventh time on the seventh day.

    iii.   Do not take anything out of the city except silver, gold, and vessels of brass and iron, which would be consecrated to the Lord.

    iv.   To destroy every person and thing inside the city, except Rahab and her family, who had helped the Israelite spies.

c.   *Sacrifice* - The Israelites had to sacrifice two very important things to receive this miracle:

    i.   They sacrificed time each day marching around the city.

    ii.   They had to refrain from taking any personal spoils after plundering the city once it had been conquered. Anything they took had to be dedicated to the Lord. Imagine having to spend seven days marching around the city, then risking your life capturing the city only to give 100% of the spoils to God!

3. *The Israelites needed to trust the plan given to Joshua.* Joshua was the only one with information from God on how the miraculous victory over Jericho was going to unfold. The Israelite people had to trust Joshua's words that the city's walls would fall if they followed his precise instructions. By following instructions, the Israelites showed great faith in their leader.

4. *The success of this miracle was due to a group effort.* All Israelites needed to participate, believe, and do his or her part for this miracle to succeed. One person failing to march, keep silence, or blow his or her trumpet, could have resulted in failure for everyone. How do we know this? The Israelite army suffered defeat due to one person's disobedience in Joshua chapter seven.

"But the children of Israel committed a trespass in the accursed thing: for Achan, the son of Carmi, the son of Zabdi, the son of Zerah, of the tribe of

Judah, took of the accursed thing: and the anger of the LORD was kindled against the children of Israel." Joshua 7:1

"Israel hath sinned, and they have also transgressed my covenant which I commanded them: for they have even taken of the accursed thing, and have also stolen, and dissembled also, and they have put *it* even among their own stuff. Therefore the children of Israel could not stand before their enemies, *but* turned *their* backs before their enemies, because they were accursed: neither will I be with you any more, except ye destroy the accursed from among you. Up, sanctify the people, and say, Sanctify yourselves against to morrow: for thus saith the LORD God of Israel, *There is* an accursed thing in the midst of thee, <u>O Israel: thou canst not stand before thine enemies, until ye take away the accursed thing from among you.</u>" Joshua 7:11-13

One person's faith (Joshua) helped galvanize the nation and secure a miraculous victory over Jericho, while a little while later, one person's foolishness was responsible for embarrassing the nation and causing loss of life. Achan's sin underscored how important it is to have unified faith in order to bring about the success of miracles.

5. *The miracle took seven days to unfold.* Most miracles in the Bible occurred in one day. The miracle of Jericho's walls falling is unique in that it took seven days of believing, marching, and silence to happen. It would have been easy for the Israelites to lose faith after two, three, or even six days, but they were determined to hold out until they received their promised miracle.

CHAPTER 4

Jesus Cures the SyroPhoenician Woman's Daughter of Demon Posession

———

The Miracle

"Then Jesus went thence, and departed into the coasts of Tyre and Sidon. And, behold, a woman of Canaan came out of the same coasts, and cried unto him, saying, Have mercy on me, O Lord, *thou* Son of David; my daughter is grievously vexed with a devil. But he answered her not a word. And his disciples came and besought him, saying, Send her away; for she crieth after us. But he answered and said, I am not sent but unto the lost sheep of the house of Israel. Then came she and worshipped him, saying, Lord, help me. But he answered and said, It is not meet to take the children's bread, and to cast *it* to dogs. And she said, Truth, Lord: yet the dogs eat of the crumbs which fall from their masters' table. Then Jesus answered and said unto her, O woman, great *is* thy faith: be it unto thee even as thou wilt. And her daughter was made whole from that very hour." Matthew 15:21-28

Reason for Choosing this Miracle

This miracle, more than any other, shows the power of determination.

Background Information

Jesus withdrew from the Israelite region of Galilee and into the Phoenician region of Tyre. Mark 7:24-30 tells us that he secretly entered a house and did not want anyone to know it. Interesting, Jesus, who came into the world to save, heal, and deliver, was now trying to hide himself! Perhaps the recent news that John the Baptist had been killed distressed him. (Matthew 14:1-12) Perhaps he was tired from feeding five thousand people who had come to him, (Matthew 14:13-21) or maybe he was tired of the endless debates with the Pharisees. (Matthew 15:1-20) Whatever the reason, Jesus wanted to be alone, but found himself confronted by another person wanting something from him. The woman encountered something no one else previously had: Jesus and his disciples refused to help her. At this point, the woman's miracle becomes extraordinary.

Key Elements of This Miracle

1. Jesus tested the woman's faith four ways before granting her request.

a. **Test #1 - Jesus refused to answer her as she asked for help.** What kind of Messiah, Savior, or healer ignores someone in need begging for help? The remarkable thing about this woman was, though Jesus ignored her, she continued pressing her case.

b. **Test #2 - The disciples of Jesus tell him to send the woman away.** Jesus had already ignored the woman, now his ministry team is shows little compassion and tells him to send her away. Most people would have definitely been so offended by the behavior of Jesus and his disciples that they would have left and probably badmouthed this ministry everywhere they went. Not this woman. She stayed and continued to press her cause.

c. **Test #3 - Jesus finally speaks to the woman and tells her he has only come to help Jewish people.** What a racist comment! Today, most people would think the woman to have definitely been justified in being upset. She might even have a valid basis for a lawsuit. So how does she handle Jesus' derogatory remarks? She hides her anger, humbles herself, kneels before Jesus and continues asking for help. (Matthew 15:25)

d. **Test #4 - Jesus equates the woman and her daughter with dogs.** Jesus says that healing this woman's daughter of demon possession would be the same as taking food away from his children and giving it to dogs. This passage of scripture seems to paint a different portrait of Jesus and the disciples because their behavior seem uncharacteristic of what we know about them. The team working with Jesus seemingly go out of their way to humiliate and get rid of this woman. She is ignored and told to go away because she and her daughter are not good enough to receive a miracle. However, despite the capricious ways that she is put-down, the woman maintains her dignity and wit. Her response to the final insult is, "Yes Lord, but the even the dogs eat the crumbs that fall from their master's table." (Matthew 15:27)

This final, remarkable response, which impressed Jesus and garnered the healing of her daughter.

"Then Jesus answered and said unto her, O woman, great *is* thy faith: be it unto thee even as thou wilt. And her daughter was made whole from that very hour." Matthew 15:28

2. *The woman cared more about her responsibility to her daughter than her right to be upset.* The woman sought Jesus out so her daughter could be healed of an evil spirit. True, she was treated unfairly, but what other choice did she have than to endure the insults? What are someone's words and opinions of us compared to divine healing? What would it have mattered for her to raise a commotion and exchange insults with Jesus and his disciples if her daughter was not healed. This woman realized that what mattered most was not the supposed insults, but the miracle she could receive. Because she endured the faith testing insults, she went home to see her daughter healed. Would you have the humility to bear similar insults if it meant that someone you loved would be healed?

3. *Great humility is equitable with great faith.* This miracle is one of only two times when Jesus commended someone for having great faith. The only other time was the centurion who considered himself unworthy for Jesus to enter his home and desired him to speak the words which would heal his servant. (Matthew 8:5-10) What do these two occasions of great faith share? Both people displayed great acts of humility. The centurion sought Jesus out, confessed his unworthiness, and prayed for his servant's healing. The woman sought Jesus out and graciously endured several insults so her daughter could be healed. Both of these people showed extraordinary faith by humbling themselves so others could be healed.

Chapter 5

The Woman with an Issue of Blood Healed

The Prayer

"And, behold, a woman, which was diseased with an issue of blood twelve years, came behind *him,* and touched the hem of his garment: For she said within herself, If I may but touch his garment, I shall be whole. But Jesus turned him about, and when he saw her, he said, Daughter, be of good comfort; thy faith hath made thee whole. And the woman was made whole from that hour." Matthew 9:20-22

Reason for Choosing this Miracle

The main reason for the selection of this miracle is that this woman was the only person in the Bible to receive an unassisted miracle, meaning she did not ask someone to heal her or pray for her sickness. Her faith was so great that it literally pulled the anointing from Jesus to heal her body.

Background Information

We do not know much about this amazing woman other than she is unnamed and her story is mentioned three times in the gospels of Matthew 9:21-22, Mark 5:25-34 and Luke 8:43-48. Luke chapter eight says that she had a chronic bleeding disorder for twelve years and spent all of her money trying to find a cure. She emphatically believed that she would be healed if she could just touch Jesus' garment.

Mark chapter five goes further in depth into her story by saying that the woman grew worse over time after trying the various unsuccessful treatments. This woman would not have had an easy life having to endure her bleeding condition as well as dealing with being ostracized from Jewish society. Leviticus 15:19-28 says that under the Law of Moses, any woman suffering from a bleeding disorder would be ritually unclean for seven days. This meant that no one could touch her or anything that she touched. These combined troubles would have made her financially, physically and emotionally broken.

Key Elements of the this Miracle

1. *This woman continued to believe, against all odds, in God's ability to heal her.* She dealt with this issue for twelve years and spent all of her money on unsuccessful a cures, only to get worse. She belonged to a religion whose laws made her an outcast

because of her sickness. Despite these things, she still believed Jesus would heal her if she could touch his clothes. Most people would have given up and embraced bitterness after going twelve without God answering their prayer, but she continued seeking after a cure. She never doubted that she would either find a cure or God would heal her. She was fully convinced of receiving a cure from God or man.

2. The woman was willing to give everything she had to receive a healing. This woman was willing to sacrifice anything to be cured. Anyone dealing a chronic sickness is willing to pay any price to more to feel normal. This woman was healed because she finally used the spiritual currency of faith, rather than financial currency. Faith is the currency of heaven and is measurable. Listen to the worlds of the Apostle Paul:

"For I say, through the grace given unto me, to every man that is among you, not to think of himself more highly than he ought to think; but to think soberly, according as God hath dealt to every man the measure of faith." Romans 12:3

Jesus confirms this in the Gospels:

"Wherefore, if God so clothe the grass of the field, which today is, and tomorrow is cast into the oven, shall he not much more clothe you, O ye of little faith? Matthew 6:30

"When Jesus heard it, he marveled, and said to them that followed, Verily I say unto you, I have not found so great faith, no, not in Israel." Matthew 8:10

"And the apostles said unto the Lord, increase our faith. And the Lord said, If ye had faith as a grain of mustard seed, ye might say unto this sycamore tree, Be thou plucked up by the root, and be thou planted in the sea; and it should obey you." Luke 17:5-6

The apostles asked Jesus to increase the faith they already had. Rather than telling them everyone has the same amount of faith, he says they only need a small amount of faith to do miraculous things. A person may not have great financial wealth, but they can have vast amounts of spiritual wealth in the form of faith. Jesus says that it only takes a small amount of faith to realize a miracle! Sometimes in order for the Lord to perform a miracle in our lives we have to realize the spiritual wealth we possess is far more important than our financial wealth.

When conventional medical treatment failed, this

woman sought an unconventional cure through faith. Divine healing often takes place when people have no other alternative but to turn to God. This usually happens because people then become willing put all of their faith and trust in Jesus when there is no other solution. We often remove God from the equation when there are other alternatives to solving our problems. Divine healing becomes a real possibility once we are willing to put all of our trust in God.

3. *The prayer that she made was short and to the point.* Matthew 9:21 tells us that the woman thought within herself that if she could just touch Jesus' clothes, she would be healed. She received a healing and did not even say her prayer aloud. This tells us that we do not always have to made loud and grandiose prayers for God to hear us. Because of her social stigma, she was probably afraid to speak in public, let alone ask Jesus to touch her. The love of God met her right where she was able to go and with what she was able to do at that time. Thank God that he meets us exactly where we are in life!

4. *Healing can take place without the man of God being aware of the person in need of a healing.* This woman's desire for healing was

so strong that she literally took power out of Jesus without his consent and into her own body to receive healing. (Mark 5:30, Luke 8:46) Most people who encountered Jesus needed him to touch them or speak a word to receive their healing. No other miracles ever came close to this woman's ability to actualize a healing without speaking to or having been touched by Jesus. This shows us that the power of God is available to anyone who believes in their heart that Jesus can heal them.

5. She needed a point of focus in order for her healing to take place. This woman had great faith, but she needed a physical object to manifest it. She could have just as easily said, "If I could just see Jesus" or "If he just looks in my direction, I will be healed." She needed to touch something before the healing could take place. When God first called Moses, he had very little faith in God and himself. This is why the Lord commanded him to use the rod in his hand to do miracles. (Exodus 4:17) Acts 5:15 tells us that multitudes of sick people were laid in the streets hoping to at least be touched by Peter's shadow that they might be healed. Acts 19:12 tells us that diseases and evil spirits departed when sick people received handkerchiefs or aprons from the Apostle Paul.

People often need something to touch in order to get their faith "over the hump" and to the place where they can manifest the miracle that they believe in God for. A good example of this is located in Mark chapter nine:

"And straightway the father of the child cried out, and said with tears, Lord, I believe; help thou mine unbelief." Mark 9:24

This man was saying, "Lord I believe that you can heal my child, but I don't know what to do to make it happen." The power of God to heal us and do miracles is always all around us. We just need the necessary faith to activate and manifest it. To pick up where we left off in story of the man with the sick child, Jesus steps in to perform the healing:

"When Jesus saw that the people came running together, he rebuked the foul spirit, saying unto him, Thou dumb and deaf spirit, I charge thee, come out of him, and enter no more into him. And the spirit cried, and rent him sore, and came out of him: and he was as one dead; insomuch that many said, He is dead. But Jesus took him by the hand, and lifted him up; and he arose." Mark 9:25-27

Jesus performs a miracle that stumped his disciples. We find out why they were not able to when they asked him how he was able to do it and they were not.

"And when he was come into the house, his disciples asked him privately, why could not we cast him out? And he said unto them, This kind can come forth by nothing, but by prayer and fasting." Mark 9:28-29

The disciples were not able to cast this particular spirit out because they did not have enough faith. The good news is that if they wanted the kind of faith that could cast troublesome spirits, they could obtain it by prayer and fasting. Sometimes a little extra is necessary to perform difficult spiritual tasks.

CHAPTER 6

Shadrach, Meshach and Abednego in the Fiery Furnace

"So these three men-Shadrach, Meshach, and Abednego-fell into the blazing furnace. They were still tied up. Then Nebuchadnezzar was startled. He sprang to his feet. He asked his advisers, "Didn't we throw three men into the fire?" "That's true, Your Majesty," they answered. The king replied, "But look, I see four men. They're untied, walking in the middle of the fire, and unharmed. The fourth one looks like a son of the gods." Then Nebuchadnezzar went to the door of the blazing furnace and said, "Shadrach, Meshach, and Abednego-servants of the Most High God-come out here." Shadrach, Meshach, and Abednego came out of the fire. The king's satraps, governors, mayors, and advisers gathered around the three men. They saw that the fire had not harmed their bodies. The hair on their heads wasn't singed, their clothes weren't burned, and they didn't smell of smoke."
Daniel 3:23-27

Reason for Choosing this Miracle

This miracle is notable because it showed how the integrity

and faith of three people resulted in miraculous deliverance and glory for God.

Background Information

Shadrach, Meshach and Abednego were carried to Babylon during the deportation of Jews in 605 BC after the fall of Jerusalem. King Nebuchadnezzar took young men from the nobility and royal families and ordered his chief official to train them for three years to serve in his palace. Shadrach, Meshach and Abednego were determined to keep their Jewish identity and resolved not to defile themselves by eating or drinking anything ritually unclean. (Daniel 1:8-15) God blessed Shadrach, Meshach and Abednego for their integrity. He gave them such impressive knowledge, understanding of literature and knowledge that the king found no one equal to them in his kingdom. In every thing Nebuchadnezzar questioned them about, he found them ten times better than all the wise men, magicians and enchanters in his kingdom. Their impressive display of wisdom and understanding garnered political prominence and favor with the king, but also attracted enemies and detractors. When Nebuchadnezzar built a large image and commanded everyone gathered to worship it, the enemies of Shadrach,

Meshach and Abednego took advantage of the opportunity and reported the three men for refusing to worship. Incensed, Nebuchadnezzar ordered that Shadrach, Meshach and Abednego be placed in the fiery furnace to see if God would deliver them.

Key Elements of This Miracle

1. *Shadrach, Meshach and Abednego refused to compromise their beliefs.* From the time that they arrived in Babylon, the three men resolved not to lose their cultural and religious identity, even if it cost them their lives. It would have been easy for them to compromise by forsaking their cultural and religious beliefs to gain favor within the royal court, but they chose to hold onto what was most valuable to them, faith in God. Jesus asked a very important question in regards to this matter:

   "For what is a man profited, if he shall gain the whole world, and lose his own soul? or what shall a man give in exchange for his soul?" Matthew 16:26

   We should consider the value of what we may lose spiritually when put in situations that call for us to compromise our religious beliefs. Shadrach, Meshach, and Abednego refused to bow down to a political authority demanding the worship of false idols. They were willing to sacrifice their lives for their beliefs and God saved them. Jesus speaks about the necessity of sacrifice in Matthew 16:24:

"Then said Jesus unto his disciples, If any *man* will come after me, let him deny himself, and take up his cross, and follow me." Matthew 16:24

Jesus sacrificed his life for us. When we become Christians, he expects us to be willing to sacrifice everything, even our lives for him. Shadrach, Meshach, and Abednego saw a great miracle because they were willing to put everything on the line and stand fast in their faith.

2. *Shadrach, Meshach, and Abednego maintained their dignity.* These men were the victims of political and racial persecution, yet they did not complain. Instead, they took the high road by having complete trust in God for their salvation. When given a second chance to recant and submit to the king's order, they gave an

interesting reply:

"Shadrach, Meshach, and Abednego, answered and said to the king, O Nebuchadnezzar, we *are* not careful to answer thee in this matter. If it be *so*, <u>our God whom we serve is able to deliver us from the burning fiery furnace, and he will deliver *us* out of thine hand, O king. But if not</u>, be it known unto thee, O king, that we will not serve thy gods, nor worship the golden image which thou hast set up." Daniel 3:16-18

They believed God could deliver them from the unjust sentence, but they were prepared in case he did not! They were fine with whatever God allowed to happen. Because they chose not to fight against false accusations, God fought for them. This showed complete trust in God.

Shadrach, Meshach and Abednego had their faith rewarded when God sent and angel to protect them. The fire in the furnace had been turned up seven times hotter and burned the soldiers who put Shadrach, Meshach, and Abednego inside, but did not burn one hair on God's faithful servants. The steadfast faith of Shadrach, Meshach, and Abednego converted Nebuchadnezzar from a pagan to a believer in the one true God. After seeing a fourth man in the fire protecting Shadrach, Meshach, and Abednego, he blessed their God and decreed that everyone should worship him (Daniel 3:28-29) In addition, Shadrach, Meshach, and Abednego were given a promotion. (Daniel 3:30) What a turnaround! Miracles and promotion await us when we stand firm and resolve to serve God, however difficult our trials and circumstances.

CHAPTER 7

Lazarus is Rises from the Dead

"Jesus said, "Take the stone away." Martha, the dead man's sister, told Jesus, "Lord, there must already be a stench. He's been dead for four days." Jesus said to her, "Didn't I tell you that if you believe, you would see God's glory?" So the stone was moved away from the entrance of the tomb. Jesus looked up and said, "Father, I thank you for hearing me. I've known that you always hear me. However, I've said this so that the crowd standing around me will believe that you sent me." After Jesus had said this, he shouted as loudly as he could, "Lazarus, come out!" The dead man came out. Strips of cloth were wound around his feet and hands, and his face was wrapped with a handkerchief. Jesus told them, "Free Lazarus, and let him go."" John 11:39-44

Reason for selecting this miracle

This miracle shows that God has the power to bring someone long dead back to life and that miracles are possible when most people doubt it.

Background Information

Lazarus and his two sisters, Martha and Mary Magdalene were friends of Jesus. Mary developed a relationship with Jesus that was closer than many of his disciples. After being healed of evil spirits and illnesses, Luke 8:1-2 says that she was part of a group of disciples who traveled from city to city with Jesus. He was close to Mary's family even stayed at their home when passing through the area. (Luke 10:38) The family sent for Jesus when Lazarus became sick. Jesus remained where he was for two days before leaving. Lazarus had been dead for more than four days by the time Jesus arrived and many thought he was well beyond any hope of being saved.

Key Elements of This Miracle

1. *Lazarus became sick and later died so God could get the glory from his resurrection.* When Jesus heard about Lazarus being sick, the Bibles says, "When Jesus heard *that,* he said, "This sickness is not unto death, but for the glory of God, that the Son of God might be glorified thereby." (John 11:4) The truth was that Jesus wanted Lazarus to die (or appear to die) so God would be glorified and people would believe in his ability to

heal. God often allows sickness and other bad things to happen as occasions for him to receive the glory when we call on him to help us. When God delivers us from our trials, it is and advertisement for his power.

2. *Jesus was always going to raise Lazarus from the dead but wanted to use the circumstances to increase the faith of others.*

"And I am glad for your sakes that I was not there, to the intent ye may believe; nevertheless let us go unto him." John 11:15

When Jesus heard that Lazarus was sick, he purposely waited two days for Lazarus expired before leaving. His disciples had a limited amount of faith, which did not extend after death. They believed only in what they saw Jesus do, such as healing and casting devils out, but they did not think that he could bring a person back from the dead after four days . . . until he proved them wrong. By arriving four days after Lazarus had died, Jesus proved his awesome power in this life and the next. He made it clear that his power was limitless.

3. *This miracle revealed the limits of Mary and Martha's faith in Christ.* Mary and Martha were ardent friends and disciples of Jesus until their brother died. They followed him from city to city, (Luke 8:1-2) hosted him in their home (Luke 10:38) and had become good friends. The sisters were clearly disappointed with Jesus when their brother died.

"Then Martha, as soon as she heard that Jesus was coming, went and met him: but Mary sat *still* in the house. Then said Martha unto Jesus, Lord, if thou hadst been here, my brother had not died." John 11:20-21

Martha goes out to meet Jesus and immediately expressed her disappointment. Her sister Mary chose to stay home and sulk. Despite her sad feelings, Martha summoned a little faith:

"But I know, that even now, whatsoever thou wilt ask of God, God will give *it* thee." John 11:22

Even with the pain of her brother's death still in her heart, Martha hoped and prayed that Jesus could revive Lazarus. When Jesus raised Lazarus from the dead, he proved that Martha was right about God giving him anything he desired. After this great miracle, Mary performs the one act, which ensured her name will live forever:

"Then Jesus six days before the Passover came to Bethany, where Lazarus was which had been dead, whom he raised from the dead. There they made him a supper; and Martha served: but Lazarus was one of them that sat at the table with him. Then took Mary a pound of ointment of spikenard, very costly, and anointed the feet of Jesus, and wiped his feet with her hair: and the house was filled with the odour of the ointment." John 12:1-3

Mary had doubted Jesus once, but never again. The world would forever know her love, faith, and commitment to Jesus Christ as she wiped his feet with her hair and tears. This is why she risked her life to stand by him at the cross, (Matthew 27:56) helped bury his body, (Mark 15:47) and watched over his grave until she was the first to see him rise from the dead. (John 20:11-15)

CHAPTER 8

Moses and the Parting of the Red Sea

"And Moses said unto the people, Fear ye not, stand still, and see the salvation of the LORD, which he will shew to you to day: for the Egyptians whom ye have seen to day, ye shall see them again no more for ever. The LORD shall fight for you, and ye shall hold your peace. And the LORD said unto Moses, Wherefore criest thou unto me? speak unto the children of Israel, that they go forward: But lift thou up thy rod, and stretch out thine hand over the sea, and divide it: and the children of Israel shall go on dry *ground* through the midst of the sea." Exodus 14:13-16

Reason for selecting this miracle

Moses parting the Red Sea is one of the most widely known miracles and was selected for three reasons:

1. It allowed an entire nation to be freed from slavery
2. The large number of people affected by this miracle, which was performed on behalf of an entire nation and destroyed the army of another.
3. The effects of this miracle reverberated for many

years, causing fear to fall on other nations that the Hebrew people faced

Background Information

The Hebrew people were the descendants promised to Abraham. God gave him a prophecy in Genesis 15:13-16 that his descendants would be slaves in a foreign land for four hundred years. God promised that he would later judge the nation who enslaved them, free the Hebrew people, and bring them back into Canaan and give it to them.

Moses was born to a Hebrew mother and adopted by Pharaoh's daughter; he grew up a Prince of Egypt, but fled after murdering an Egyptian man for abusing a Hebrew slave. He was eighty years when God called him to return to Egypt, deliver his people from slavery, and bring them into the Promised Land. God used Moses to bring ten devastating plagues on Egypt and force Pharaoh to free the Hebrew people. As Moses and the Hebrews left, Pharaoh changed his mind and assembled his army to pursue his former slaves. It was at the shores of the Red Sea where the Egyptian army overtook the Hebrews and God began to perform miracles.

Key Elements of This Miracle

1. *God wanted to deliver his people, but also wanted to be exalted in the sight of the Hebrews, Pharaoh and the Egyptians.*

"And I will harden Pharaoh's heart, that he shall follow after them; and I will be honoured upon Pharaoh, and upon all his host; that the Egyptians may know that I *am* the LORD. And they did so." Exodus 14:4

God displayed his awesome power and greatness when he parted the Red Sea and destroyed Pharaoh's army. God will sometimes allow us to fall into circumstances that only he can save us from so we are forced to call on him for deliverance. When the Lord does deliver us, he alone will get the glory and others will know the greatness of our God. The Hebrew people had spent four hundred years as slaves in a foreign land and forgot whom the God of Abraham, Isaac and Jacob really was. They feared their Egyptian masters and their pagan gods, knowing nothing about God's divine power, love, mercy, and grace until he delivered them through miracles.

The Hebrews would have had good reason to fear. Pharaohs' magicians possessed what seemed like supernatural power. They matched Moses and Aaron miracle for miracle, plague for plague, up to a certain point. The magicians duplicated the first miracles Moses performed of changing Aaron's rod into a snake (Exodus 7:11-12) and turning water into blood. (Exodus 7:22) After that, the magicians failed to reproduce Moses' miracles and had to admit that the God of the Hebrews had superior power. God needed to do this to show his people that he was the one true God who they should trust in as their ultimate savior. Many people will never be convinced that Jesus is Lord and savior with arguments and debate. Only the miracles of God will turn them toward the truth.

2. *This miracle began with the prayers and cries of the Hebrew people.*

"And it came to pass in process of time, that the king of Egypt died: and the children of Israel sighed by reason of the bondage, and they cried, and their cry came up unto God by reason of the bondage. <u>And God heard their groaning, and God remembered his covenant with Abraham, with Isaac, and with Jacob. And God looked upon the children of Israel, and God had respect unto them.</u>" Exodus 2:23-25

It took a long time, but God eventually heard the groaning and prayers of his people and decided to deliver them. Four hundred years had passed since God's covenant with Abraham and his promise to free them from slavery. If they had not cried out to God during their bondage, they might have remained in slavery much longer, perhaps four hundred and fifty years or longer. Their prayers caused God to have compassion on them at that time and served as a reminder that he was obligated to keep the agreement he made with Abraham.

3. *God performed this miracle to free the Hebrew people so they could worship and serve him.*

    "And thou shalt say unto him, The LORD God of the Hebrews hath sent me unto thee, saying, <u>Let my people go, that they may serve me</u> in the wilderness: and, behold, hitherto thou wouldest not hear." Exodus 7:16

The word "worship" used here also means "serve" in the Gods Word Translation of the Bible. God wants us to worship and serve him and will perform miracles if someone is denying us the right to worship him to help us get to a place where we can. When he performs the miracle, he expects us to worship him.

4. *Another miracle was necessary for this miracle to take place.* The parting of the Red sea was the second of two miracles needed to give the Hebrew people freedom from the Egyptians. Pharaoh and his army pursued the Hebrew people to the Red Sea and would have captured them if God had not stopped them.

"And the angel of God, which went before the camp of Israel, removed and went behind them; and the pillar of the cloud went from before their face, and stood behind them: And it came between the camp of the Egyptians and the camp of Israel; and it was a cloud and darkness *to them,* but it gave light by night *to these:* so that the one came not near the other all the night. And Moses stretched out his hand over the sea; and the LORD caused the sea to go *back* by a strong east wind all that night, and made the sea dry *land,* and the waters were divided." Exodus 14:19-21

God sent his angel and cloud of glory to stand between the Hebrew people and the Egyptians in order to make sure that his people made it to safety. Why did God allow the Egyptians to come so close to recapturing the Hebrew people? Exodus 14:13-16 tells us why:

"And Moses said unto the people, Fear ye not, stand still, and see the salvation of the LORD, which he will shew to you to day: for the Egyptians whom ye have seen to day, ye shall see them again no more for ever. The LORD shall fight for you, and ye shall hold your peace. And the LORD said unto Moses, Wherefore criest thou unto me? speak unto the children of Israel, that they go forward: But lift thou up thy rod, and stretch out thine hand over the sea, and divide it: and the children of Israel shall go on dry *ground* through the midst of the sea." Exodus 14:13-16

God did it for two reasons:

1. To test the faith of his people and see if they would call on him.

2. To lure the Egyptian army into a trap so he could destroy any capability they would have of causing his people any trouble in the future. When God destroyed Pharaoh and his army, his people were free to worship and serve him the way he wanted. When the Lord does a miracle in our lives, he desires to give us complete victory so we will never again have to worry about experiencing the same predicament. This is complete deliverance.

CHAPTER 9

Elijah and the Prophets of Baal

"And it came to pass at *the time of* the offering of the *evening* sacrifice, that Elijah the prophet came near, and said, LORD God of Abraham, Isaac, and of Israel, let it be known this day that thou *art* God in Israel, and *that* I *am* thy servant, and *that* I have done all these things at thy word. Hear me, O LORD, hear me, that this people may know that thou *art* the LORD God, and *that* thou hast turned their heart back again. Then the fire of the LORD fell, and consumed the burnt sacrifice, and the wood, and the stones, and the dust, and licked up the water that *was* in the trench. And when all the people saw *it,* they fell on their faces: and they said, The LORD, he *is* the God; the LORD, he *is* the God." 1 Kings 18:36-39

Reason for selecting this miracle

Elijah was one of a handful of people who spiritually revived an entire nation in one day. The miracle he performed revived the nation of Israel and converted people from worshipping pagans to serving the one true God.

Background Information

Elijah was one of the greatest prophets of the Bible. He was one of two men to have never died (the other was Enoch in Genesis 5:24) and had the privilege of reappearing to converse with Jesus during his New Testament ministry. (Matthew 17:3) Elijah carried such a powerful anointing that a dead man revived back to life after touching Elijah's bones. (2 Kings 13:21)

Elijah emerged from hiding to perform this great miracle. King Ahab and his wife Queen Jezebel had forcefully removed Mosaic Law and set up their pagan religion. Ahab issued a death warrant against Elijah for decrying his spiritual wickedness and prophesying a drought upon Israel. Elijah fled to Zarephath in Phoenicia and hid for three and a half years until God told him to return to Israel, confront Ahab, and bring rain upon the earth. Elijah confronted Ahab and proposed that he gather all of Israel at Mount Carmel for a spiritual showdown against four hundred and fifty prophets of Baal and four hundred prophets of the grove. Under these dire circumstances, Elijah performed his greatest miracle.

Key Elements of This Miracle

1. *Elijah performed this miracle by following instructions from God.*

> "And it came to pass at *the time of* the offering of the *evening* sacrifice, that Elijah the prophet came near, and said, LORD God of Abraham, Isaac, and of Israel, let it be known this day that thou *art* God in Israel, and *that* I *am* thy servant, and *that* I have done all these things at thy word." 1 Kings 18:36

God told Elijah to confront Ahab and rain would soon follow. (1 Kings 18:1) The idea to assemble the prophets of Baal, the grove, and all of Israel at Mount Carmel came from God. Elijah may have devised the specifics, like what to put on the altar, or pouring barrels of water on his sacrifice, but the orders came from God. Elijah had faith that if he defeated and humiliated the false prophets, people would return from idolatry. Elijah's faith shows how one person under God's anointing could turn an entire nation from false religion to truth by obeying God.

2. *Elijah built and altar to honor Abraham's covenant
    agreements and restore the traditional way that God instructed
    his people to worship before attempting this miracle.*

"And Elijah said unto all the people, Come near
unto me. And all the people came near unto him. And
he repaired the altar of the LORD *that was* broken
down. And Elijah took twelve stones, according to the
number of the tribes of the sons of Jacob, unto
whom the word of the LORD came, saying, Israel
shall be thy name: And with the stones he built an
altar in the name of the LORD: and he made a trench
about the altar, as great as would contain two
measures of seed." 1 Kings 18:30-32

When Elijah repaired the abandoned altar, he was
symbolically repairing the spiritual relationship
between God and his people. He did something that
Israel's ancestors had done when they wanted to
honor God for his covenants through sacrifice. This
was a spiritual pattern in the history of Israel's
ancestors:

A. (Genesis 8:20-21) The first thing Noah did after spending nearly a year aboard the ark was to build an altar and make sacrifices. As a result, God made a covenant with him not to destroy the world by water again.

B. (Genesis 12:7, 13:18, 22:9) Abraham built altars and sacrificed to God three times in his life after the Lord blessed him and made covenants.

C. (Genesis 26:23-25) Isaac built an altar to show that he would honor his fathers covenant after God appeared to him in Beersheba.

D. (Genesis 33:20, 35:1) Jacob built two altars to God and worshipped during times of distress in his life.

E. (Exodus 17:14-16) Moses built and altar to signify God's covenant with Israel after a trying battle against the Amalakites.

F. (Judges 6:24-32) Gideon cast down the altar of Baal and built an altar to the Lord to signify that he was restoring the traditional Mosaic law of worship.

Whenever someone wanted to honor

God, renew their spiritual relationship with him, remind God of their covenant, or call on the Lord for deliverance, they built and altar and sacrificed. Elijah did this to show God that he was serious about the Lord performing a miracle and turning the hearts of Israel back to him. Even before Jesus spoke the words in the New Testament, Elijah understood that God desires his people to worship him in Spirit and in truth. (John 4:24)

3. *Elijah was bold enough to worship God when no one else would.*

"And Elijah came unto all the people, and said, How long halt ye between two opinions? if the LORD *be* God, follow him: but if Baal, *then* follow him. And the people answered him not a word. Then said Elijah unto the people, I, *even* I only, remain a prophet of the LORD; but Baal's prophets *are* four hundred and fifty men." 1 Kings 18:21-22

Elijah asked the people whether they would serve Baal or the true God, but no one was willing to answer him. He boldly stood alone against the king of

Israel and eight hundred and fifty false prophets in the sight of the entire nation to declare his dedication to God. If we want to see miracles as servants of God, then we have to be willing to stand up for him when no on else will. God's mightiest servants have always been bold in the willingness to serve him. The Apostle Paul declares that true power with God lies in not being ashamed of him:

"<u>For I am not ashamed</u> of the gospel of Christ: for <u>it is the power of God unto salvation</u> to every one that believeth; to the Jew first, and also to the Greek." Romans 1:16

"For God hath not given us the spirit of fear; but of power, and of love, and of a sound mind. <u>Be not thou therefore ashamed of the testimony of our Lord</u>, nor of me his prisoner: but be thou partaker of the afflictions of the <u>gospel according to the power of God</u>;" 2 Timothy 1:7-8

The key to defeating the fear and shame that sometimes comes upon us when we want to proclaim Christ diminishes when we rely on the Holy Spirit to embolden us. Paul tells us in 2 Timothy 1:7 that God's Spirit gives us the power, love and mind to do what needs to be done for God. Elijah performed his greatest miracle by relying on the power of God's Spirit.

4. *Elijah's prayer gave God a reason to act.*

"Hear me, O LORD, hear me, that this people may know that thou *art* the LORD God, and *that* thou hast turned their heart back again." 1 Kings 18:37

Elijah stood before the altar and prayed with a purpose. He wanted God to do two specific things:

1. For people to know the God he served was the true God.
2. For God to turn the hearts of Israel back to the true God.

Elijah was at Mount Carmel to confront Ahab and bring rain. Turning the people back to God was something extra that he wanted to accomplish. This is similar to the time when God visited Abraham before destroying Sodom and Gomorrah searching for an intercessor. (Genesis 18) God could have let the angels destroy the cities without stopping by to speak with his friend. There was no reason for God to visit Abraham in person other than to see if Abraham would act as an intercessor and bargain for condemned souls. God desires humanity to turn back to him and looks for intercessors to work through.

"And I sought for a man among them, that should make up the hedge, and stand in the gap before me for the land, that I should not destroy it: but I found none." Ezekiel 22:30

"And he saw that *there was* no man, and wondered that *there was* no intercessor: therefore his arm brought salvation unto him; and his righteousness, it sustained him." Isaiah 59:16

5. *This miracle cost Elijah personally and spiritually.* The people of Israel reaped the rewards of rain and spiritual renewal brought about by Elijah's faith, but he was the one who paid the price. First, it cost him his reputation. After Elijah performed miracles, Queen Jezebel issued a death warrant against him. (1

Kings 19:1-3) Second, he alone had to summon the faith, courage, and boldness to stand before King Ahab, the false prophets and all of Israel to repair the altar of the Lord and declare his name. The life of the man of God is often a lonely and underappreciated walk, but thank God, someone is willing to do it, or who would be saved?

Chapter 10

Jehoshaphat's Miraculous Deliverance from Ammonite and
Moabite Armies

———

"And they rose early in the morning, and went forth into the wilderness of Tekoa: and as they went forth, Jehoshaphat stood and said, Hear me, O Judah, and ye inhabitants of Jerusalem; Believe in the LORD your God, so shall ye be established; believe his prophets, so shall ye prosper. And when he had consulted with the people, he appointed singers unto the LORD, and that should praise the beauty of holiness, as they went out before the army, and to say, Praise the LORD; for his mercy *endureth* for ever. And when they began to sing and to praise, the LORD set ambushments against the children of Ammon, Moab, and mount Seir, which were come against Judah; and they were smitten. For the children of Ammon and Moab stood up against the inhabitants of mount Seir, utterly to slay and destroy *them*: and when they had made an end of the inhabitants of Seir, every one helped to destroy another. And when Judah came toward the watch tower in the wilderness, they looked unto the multitude, and, behold, they *were* dead bodies fallen to the earth, and none escaped. And when Jehoshaphat and his people came to take away the spoil of them, they found among them in abundance both riches with the dead bodies, and precious jewels, which they stripped off for themselves, more than they could carry away: and they were three days in gathering of the spoil, it was so much." 2 Chronicles 20:20-25

Reason for selecting this miracle

This miracle was selected because it shows the power of a political figure, King Jehoshaphat, uniting his nation in prayer and fasting to miraculously defeat several invading nations. Thousands of people were affected by this miracle and it showed a complete reversal of fortune where the nation of Judah went from being desperately outnumbered to receiving victory and great financial blessings.

Background Information about this Miracle

Jehoshaphat was the king of Judah and prayed for God to save his country from a large invading coalition of Moabite, Ammonite and other enemy forces. Jehoshaphat was the fourth king of Judah and a direct descendant of David. His nation had become a strong military power and was firmly established in the Middle East. He had great wealth and honor because the people of Judah and surrounding nations brought gifts and tribute to him. 2 Chronicles 20:10 says that the fear of the Lord fell on all the kingdoms surrounding Judah. No one had dared to make war against Judah out of respect for their status and military power up until the time the Moabites and Ammonites led a coalition against them.

Jehoshaphat made the mistake marrying the daughter of Ahab, the wicked king of Israel, to form an alliance. The prophet Jehu told Jehoshaphat that the wrath of God would come on him for foolishly allying himself with Ahab. The large invasion Jehoshaphat now faced was the result of the word that God spoke against him for his foolish actions.

Key Elements of Jehoshaphat's Miracle

1. Jehoshaphat was willing to ask for help when he needed it.
Jehoshaphat realized the situation he faced was beyond his control and chose to ask God for help. He realized his poor judgment in the past and was now humble and wise enough to seek the Lord's help in defending his nation against overwhelming odds. Many leaders and ordinary people are not willing to humble themselves and ask for God's help in hopeless situations. Instead, many people hopelessly try to

solve extreme problems on their own. If a problem is extremely complex or overwhelming, why not seek God's help? He created the entire universe, formed our little planet in six days and our frail, human body in one day. There are no problem too big for God! We should never fear admitting that a problem is too big for us. Asking for help does not mean that we are somehow inadequate; it means that we are human. Some of life's problems are just too big for us and we need a big God to help us.

2. *Jehoshaphat realized that his problem was the result of spiritual consequences.* The invasion Jehoshaphat faced was linked to the wrath that Jehu prophesied to come upon him. This was spiritual consequence of poor decision-making. Jehoshaphat wisely realized that since his problem began and ended with God, he needed God's help solving it.

3. *Jehoshaphat reminded God of his greatness and power.* Worshipping God and exalting him for his magnificence and power should be the primary focus of any prayer. We must realize that we were created with the intent of glorifying God. (Isaiah 43:7) Because we are God's creation, he is more inclined to aid us when we fulfill our primary purpose of

worshipping than when we do not worship him. Giving God glory and honor motivates Him to show us favor.

God is not under any obligation to intervene in the affairs of humanity. He created the world, died on the cross and paid the penalty for our sins. Anything extra that he provides should be viewed as God's favor and blessings. We should rouse him into action with the proper love, praise and adoration in our prayers. We are trying to please God, not a common person. He should be more highly esteemed than our celebrities, kings and heads of state. The proper way to approach God is from a point of humility and reverence as Jehoshaphat did with his awe-inspiring prayer that lifted God as the Creator and supreme ruler of the universe. Psalms 29:2 puts worshipping God in the proper perspective:

"Give unto the LORD the glory due unto his name; worship the LORD in the beauty of holiness." Psalms 29:2

We praise God, not because he owes us something, but because we owe him the glory. We are breathing his air. . . . his sunlight shines on us through his sky as we stand on his planet. Sometimes we forget all that God has done and is doing when we have pressing issues on our mind when we are praying. God remains glorious, magnificent and on the throne throughout our difficulties. As we begin to praise him for his great power and glory, if we put him in his proper place, miraculous things will begin to occur. We will see that God is bigger than our problems when we uplift him instead of our problems. When Jehoshaphat magnified God, he knew the Lord could turn back any army. Worshipping and glorifying God in prayer minimizes the issues we are facing and maximizes the Lord's ability to solve it.

4. Jehoshaphat reaffirmed his nation's right to exist and worship God. Judah was being threatened with invasion. This meant several things. First, the people of Judah would have lost control of the land that God gave to their ancestors. Second, if they were conquered, they would not be able to serve God the way that they wanted. In Jehoshaphat's mind, God should be offended by people who dared to take away the blessings he had given Israel. Jehoshaphat prayed knowing the people of Judah were God's children and the Moabites and Amorites were trying to harm them. What father would not feel rage against someone trying to harm his defenseless children? Jehoshaphat knew that by praying to God as a Father and protector, miraculous deliverance had to happen.

Jehoshaphat tells the people in 2 Chronicles 20:15 that the battle was not theirs, but God's. Many trials that we encounter in life are not a personal attack on us, but have to do with our identity as people of God. The enemy fights to take away what God has blessed us with or will bless us with in the future. Victory is nearby when we realize that many of our battles do not belong to us and should not be fought by us. Our responsibility is to let God fight the battle through us by shifting spiritual command to him in prayer.

5. Jehoshaphat had no doubt that God was going to answer his prayer. Jehoshaphat continued to pray and expect a miracle from God, though he had been cursed for making foolish choices. Jehoshaphat understood that past mistakes do not necessarily determine present deliverance. God is merciful and the calling on him with the right prayers can soften his heart. David said this about calling out to the Lord in a time of trouble:

"The righteous cry, and the LORD heareth, and delivereth them out of all their troubles. The LORD is nigh unto them that are of a broken heart; and saveth such as be of a contrite spirit. Many are the afflictions of the righteous: but the LORD delivereth him out of them all." Psalms 34:17-19

Jehoshaphat's deliverance came about because of understanding how to pray and what to say. Showing humility, worshipping God with a broken heart, contrite spirit, and including certain aspects of Israel's history roused God into acting favorably on Judah's behalf. How could he turn his people away with the kind of petition they made with prayer and fasting? Jehoshaphat told the people in 2 Chronicles 20:20 that when they have faith in God and his prophets, success will follow. Jehoshaphat believed their triumph and deliverance was as good as done when he finished praying. He told the people in verse twenty-one to praise and worship God as their army went out to battle. Their faith was evident because they praised God for what he was going to do before it happened. If you really trust that God will answer your prayer, don't wait until the struggle is over...praise him in the midst of it!

God responded to their faith. 2 Chronicles 20:22 says the Lord set ambushes against the enemy and defeated them.

Verse twenty-three says that the enemy rose and destroyed one another. When Judah arrived at the site of the battle, they did not have to fight because the enemy was already defeated. In addition, a vast amount of wealth, equipment, clothing, and other valuable items was left behind by the enemy…more than Judah could take away. It took three days to collect it all! Jehoshaphat and the people of Judah went from being in fear of their lives and possibly losing everything to being victorious and gaining more financial wealth than they could carry. This was a complete reversal of fortune. We should not fear trials because God can miraculously deliver us when we put our complete trust in him. A spiritual or financial blessing often accompanies the end of our trial as God's reward for trusting in him. Several scriptures tell us that God can do more than we ask when we go through trials and pray:

"Thou preparest a table before me in the presence of mine enemies: thou anointest my head with oil; my cup runneth over." Psalms 23:5

"Now unto him that is able to do exceeding abundantly above all that we ask or think, according to the power that worketh in us." Ephesians 3:20

Jehoshaphat's great miracle teaches us that we should not be dismayed when faced with overwhelming trouble because God can turn our troubles into deliverance and overwhelming blessings.

∞

If would like to be updated about the future release of books by Benjamin L. Reynolds, please email info@benjaminlreynolds.com or visit www.benjaminlreynolds.com to be added to our mailing list

Appendix 1: All the Miracles in the Bible and their Types

I   Miracles Involving the Human Body

1.   Miraculous Pregnancy/Birth (7 times, 5 OT/2 NT)

     a.   (Gen. 21:1-8) Birth of Isaac

     b.   Birth of Joseph (Genesis 29:31, 30:22-24)

     c.   (Judges 13:3-25) Birth of Samson

     d.   Birth of Samuel (1 Samuel 1:6-20)

     e.   (2 Kings 4:11-18) Shunammite woman conceives a son

     f.   (Luke 1:5-60) Birth of John the Baptist

     g.   (Luke 1:30-35) Conception and Birth of Jesus

2.   Miraculous conception and birth of a child (7 Times, 6 OT/1 NT)

     a.   Birth of Sampson (Judges 13)

     b.   Birth of Jesus (Luke 1:5-25, 57-66)

     c.

3.   Disease Cured

     a.   Leprosy cured (4 times, 2 OT/2 NT)

      i. (Numbers 12:12-15) Miriam healed of leprosy after 7 days

      ii. (2 Kings 5:10-27) Naaman healed of leprosy

      iii. (Luke 17:11-19) Ten lepers healed

      iv. (Matt 8:2; Mark 1:40; Luke 5:12) Leper healed

b. Healed of snake bites (2 times, 1 OT/1 NT)

      i. (Numbers 21:8-9) People healed of snake bites after looking at bronze serpent

      ii. (Acts 28:3-6) Paul healed of snake bite

c. Resurrection from dead (7 times, 3 OT/4 NT)

      i. (1 Kings 17:17-24) Widows son raised from the dead

      ii. (2 Kings 4:32-37) Shunammite woman's sons raised from dead

      iii. (2 Kings 13:21) Man revived after touching Elisha's bones

       iv. (Matthew 9:23, Mark 5:23, Luke 8:41) Jairus' daughter raised

       v. (Luke 7:11-18) Widow's son in funeral procession at Nain revived

      vi. (John 11:38-44) Lazerus raised from the dead after 3 days

     vii. (John 21:1-14) The resurrection of Jesus

d. Miracles involving restoration of sight, blindness (7 times, 2 OT, 5 NT)

       i. 2 Kings 6:17 Gehazi's eyes opened to see angelic army at Dothan

      ii. 2 Kings 6:20 The Syrian army cured of blindness at Samaria

     iii. (Matt 9:27-31) Cure of two blind men

      iv. (Mark 8:22-26) The blind man of Bethsaida

      v. (John 9:1-7) Man born blind cured

      vi. (Matt 20:29; Mark 10:46; Luke 18:35) Two blind men cured

     vii. (Acts 9:8-9, 18) Paul's sight restored

e. Healing of the inability to speak or hear (2 times, 2 NT)

    i. (Mark 7:31-37) Deaf and dumb man healed

    ii. (Matt 12:22; Luke 11:14) Blind and dumb demoniac cured

f. Withered hand healed (2 times, 1 OT/1 NT)

    i. (1 Kings 13:4-6) Jeroboam's withered hand healed

    ii. (Matt 12:10; Mark 3:1; Luke 6:6)Man's withered hand cured

g. (Luke 14:1-6) Man healed of dropsy (excess bodily fluid)

h. People with issues of paralysis (7 times, 7 NT)

    i. (Luke 13:11-17) The woman with the spirit of infirmity cured

    ii. (John 5:1-9) Impotent man at Bethsaida cured

    iii. (Matt 9:2; Mark 2:3; Luke 5:18) Man sick of the palsy cured

iv. (Acts 3:2-8) Peter heals paralyzed man

v. (Acts 14:8-10) Paul heals lame man at Lystra

vi. (Acts 19:11-12) People were healed and freed of demonic possession by touching handkerchiefs which had touched Paul's body

i. Demonic possession cured (3 Times, 3 NT)

  i. (Matt 15:28; Mark 7:24) Syrophoenician woman's daughter cured

  ii. (Matt 8:28; Mark 5:1; Luke 8:26) Demoniacs of Gadara cured

  iii. (Matt 17:14; Mark 9:14; Luke 9:37) A lunatic child cured

j. (Luke 22:50-51) Malchus' severed ear put back in place

k. (2 Kings 20:1-11, Isaiah 38:1-5) Hezekiah healed of life threatening boil

l. (Acts 28:7-8) Paul heals Publius of fever and dysentery at Malta

m. General sickness healed (4 Times, 4 NT)

    i. (John 4:46-54) Cure of nobleman's son, Capernaum

    ii. (Matthew 8:5; Luke 7:1) Centurion's servant healed

    iii. (Matthew 8:14; Mark 1:30; Luke 4:38) Peter's wife's mother cured

    iv. (John 5:2-4) Angel who healed sicknesses at Bethesda

4. The human body supernaturally changed or enhanced (4 times, 3 OT/1 NT)

a. (Judges 14-16) Samson's Superhuman strength

b. (1 Kings 18:46) Elijah given supernatural speed and endurance

c. (1 Kings 19:5-8) Elijah's body supernaturally enhanced for 40 days and night after eating bread and water provided by angel of the Lord

d. (Matthew 17:1-8) The transfiguration of Jesus

II   Miracles of Nature

1. (Exodus 3:3)The burning bush not consumed
2. (Ex. 7:10-12)Aaron's rod changed into a serpent
3. The ten plagues of Egypt
    a. (Exodus 7:20-12:30) Waters become blood
    b. (Ex. 7:20-12:30) Frogs
    c. (Ex. 7:20-12:30) Lice
    d. (Ex. 7:20-12:30) Flies
    e. (Ex. 7:20-12:30) Livestock Disease
    f. (Ex. 7:20-12:30) Boils
    g. (Ex. 7:20-12:30) Thunder and hail
    h. (Ex. 7:20-12:30) Locusts
    i. (Ex. 7:20-12:30) Darkness
    j. (Ex. 7:20-12:30) Death of the first-born
4. Sea or river divided (2 Times, 2 OT)
    a. (Ex. 14:21-31) Red Sea divided by Moses
    b. (Josh. 3:14-17) The Jordan divided, so that Israel passed over
5. Water purified (2 times, 2 OT)
    a. (Ex. 15:23-25) Waters of Marah sweetened
    b. (2 Kings 2:21, 22) Waters of Jericho healed when Elisha's put salt into them

6. Miraculous appearance/disappearance of water (5 times, 4 OT)

    a. (Ex. 17:5-7) Water from the rock at Rephidim

    b. (Num. 20:7-11) Water from the rock, smitten twice by Moses, desert of Zin

    c. (Judg. 15:19) Water from a hollow place in Lehi

    d. (1 Kings 17:1) Elijah prophesies no rain until he speaks it

    e. (2 Kings 3:16-20) Water provided for Jehoshaphat and the allied army

7. (Num. 17:8) Aaron's rod budding at Kadesh

8. (Josh. 6:6-20) The walls of Jericho fall down

9. Celestial Bodies (3 times, 2 OT/1 NT)

    a. (Josh. 10:12-14)The sun and moon stand still

    b. (2 Kings 20:1-11) Hezekiah healed and shadow on sun dial goes back ten degrees

    c. (Matthew 2:1-10) Star guiding wise men to Jesus

10. (1 Sam. 5:1-12) Dagon falls twice before the ark.

11. Rain and Thunderstorms (3 Times, 3 OT)

a. (1 Sam. 7:10-12) Thunderstorm causes a panic among the Philistines at Eben-ezer

b. (1 Sam. 12:18) Thunder and rain in harvest at Gilgal

c. (1 Kings 18:41-45) Elijah prays for rain

12. (1 Kings 17, 18) Drought at Elijah's prayers

13. Miracles involving Fire (3 Times, 3 OT)

a. (1 Kings 18:19-39) Fire from heaven at Elijah's prayers

b. (2 Kings 1:10-12) Fire falls from the sky and consumes two groups of fifty soldiers

c. (Dan. 3:10-27) Shadrach, Meshach, and Abed-nego delivered from the fiery furnace, Babylon

14. Defiance of Gravity (3 Times, 1 OT/2 NT)

a. (2 Kings 6:5-7) Iron axe-head floats

b. (Matt 14:25; Mark 6:48; John 6:15) Jesus walks on water

c. (Matthew 14:29-30) Peter walks on Water

15. (Judg. 6:37-40) Gideon's fleece

16. (Matt 21:18; Mark 11:12) Fig tree withered

17. (Matt 8:23; Mark 4:37; Luke 8:22) Jesus calms the storm

18. Apostles free from prison (3 times, 3 NT)

    a. (Acts 5:19) The apostles freed from prison by an earthquake

    b. (Acts 16:26) Paul and Silas freed from prison by an earthquake

    c. (Acts 12:3-11) Paul and Silas freed from prison by an angel

III   Military Miracles of Deliverance (5 times, 5 OT)

1. (2 Sam. 5:23-25)Sound in the mulberry trees at Rephaim

2. (2 Kings 19:35) Sennacherib's army destroyed, Jerusalem

3. (2 Kings 6:18) The Syrian army smitten with blindness at Dothan

4. (2 Kings 19) 185,000 Assyrians killed by the angel of the Lord after Hezekiah prays for deliverance

5. (2 Chronicles 20) The LORD set ambushes against the Ammonites, Moabites, and people of Mount Seir as Jehoshaphat and Israel worship and sing praises

III   Miracles Involving Food (10 times 6 OT/4 NT)

1. (Ex. 16:14-35) Manna sent everyday, except on the Sabbath
2. (1 Kings 17, 18) Elijah fed by ravens
3. Widow of Zarephath's meal and oil increased (1 Kings 17:14-16)
4. (2 Kings 4:38-41)The deadly pottage cured with meal at Gilgal
5. (2 Kings 4:42-44) A hundred men fed with twenty loaves at Gilgal
6. (1 Kings 19:5-8) Angel of the Lord gives Elijah bread and water
7. (John 2:1-11) Water made wine
8. (John 21:1-14) Large catch of fish
9. (Matt 15:32; Mark 8:1) Four thousand fed
10. (Matt 14:15; Mark 6:30; Luke 9:10; John 6:1-14) Jesus feeds 5,000

IV   Miracles Involving Animals (4 times 4 OT)

1. (Num. 22:21-35) Balaam's donkey speaks
2. (Dan. 6:16-23) Daniel saved in the lions' den
3. (Jonah 2:1-10) Jonah in the fish's belly

V   Financial Miracles (2 times 1 OT/1 NT)

1. (2 Kings 4:2-7) The widow's oil multiplied

2. (Matt 17:24-27) Piece of money in the fish's mouth